Search
and Solve

Other books by Betty De Vries

101 Bible Activity Sheets
Bible Activity Sheets for Special Days, with Mary Loeks

Search and Solve

Bible Activity Sheets

Betty De Vries

Illustrated by Donna Greenlee

 Baker Books

A Division of Baker Book House Co
Grand Rapids, Michigan 49516

Published by Baker Books
a division of Baker Book House Company
P.O. Box 6287, Grand Rapids, MI 49516-6287

Printed in the United States of America

ISBN 0-8010-5770-1

For current information about all releases from Baker Book House, visit our web
site:

http://www.bakerbooks.com

Contents

Old Testament Stories

New Testament Stories

Miscellaneous Activities

Old Testament
Stories

1. In the Beginning

All of the words in the first verse of the Bible belong in this stack-a-word puzzle. See if you can fit them in.

IN   THE
THE   HEAVENS
BEGINNING   AND
GOD   THE
CREATED   EARTH

2. Talking Animals

Animals do not talk so humans can understand them, yet twice in the Bible an animal did speak to humans. Connect the dots and then color the two animals who spoke. You can read about these talking animals in Genesis 3 and Numbers 22.

3. What to Eat

Long ago the Israelites were told which animals and insects they could eat and which ones they should not eat. Only the first letter of each animal is given here. Read Leviticus 11:22, 29–30 and complete the list. Then use all the animal names in the stack-a-word puzzle on the next page.

Not Okay to Eat

W _ _ _ _ _

G _ _ _ _

C _ _ _ _ _ _ _

L _ _ _ _ _

S _ _ _ _

R _ _

Okay to Eat

L _ _ _ _ _

C _ _ _ _ _ _

K _ _ _ _ _ _

G _ _ _ _ _ _ _ _ _

4. Ten Plagues

God sent ten plagues on Egypt before Pharaoh would let the Israelites leave. In Psalm 78, a psalm writer describes the plagues. Fill in the blanks below to find the names of things hidden in the picture on the next page.

He turned their rivers to blood;
　they could not drink from their _____.
He sent swarms of _____ that devoured them
　and _____ that devastated them.
He gave their crops to the _____,
　their produce to the _____.
He destroyed their _____ with hail
　and their sycamore-figs with sleet.
He gave over their _____ to the _____,
　their livestock to bolts of _____.

Psalm 78:44–48

5. Moses' Song

After Pharaoh's army was destroyed in the Red Sea, Moses sang a song of thanks to God. Here are parts of it in code. If you need help, read Exodus 15:1–5.

2/A	3/B	5/C	7/D	9/E	11/F	13/G
15/H	17/I	19/J	21/K	23/L	25/M	
27/N	29/O	31/P	33/Q	35/R	37/S	
39/T	41/U	43/V	45/W	47/X	49/Y	51/Z

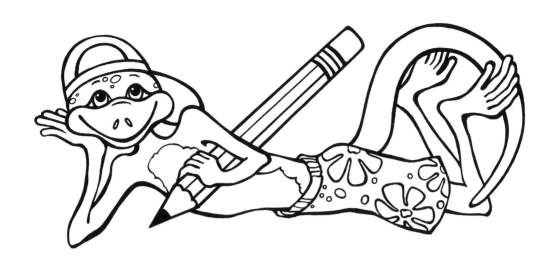

 ___ ____ ___ ___ ___   ____ ___ ___ ___   ____ ___   ____ ___ __
 17   45   17   23   23   37   17   27   13   39   29   39   15   9

 ___ ___ ___ __ , ___ ___ ___   ___ __   ___ ___
 23   29   35   7   11   29   35   15   9   17   37

 ___ ___ ___ ___ ___ ___   __ ___ __ ___ ___ __ __ .
 15   17   13   15   23   49   9   47   2   23   39   9   7

 ___ ___ __   ___ ___ ___ ___ __   __ ___ __   ___ ___ ___
 39   15   9   15   29   35   37   9   2   27   7   17   39   37

 ___ ___ __ __ ___   ___ __   ___ __ ___   ___ ___ ___ ___ __ __
 35   17   7   9   35   15   9   15   2   37   15   41   35   23   9   7

 ___ ___ ___ ___   ___ ___ __   ___ __ __ . . . .   ___ ___ __
 17   27   39   29   39   15   9   37   9   2   39   15   9

                                                                    ,
 __ __ ___ ___   ___ ___   ___ ___ __ ___ __ ___ ___ ___
 3   9   37   39   29   11   31   15   2   35   2   29   15   37

 ___ ___ ___ ___ __ __ ___ ___
 29   11   11   17   5   9   35   37

 __ ___ __   __ ___ ___ ___ ___ __ __
 2   35   9   7   35   29   45   27   9   7

 ___ ___   ___ ___ __   ___ __ __   ___ __ __ .
 17   27   39   15   9   35   9   7   37   9   2

6. A Trail of Letters

For forty years the Israelites wandered in the desert. Form words about their experience from the trail of letters below. Write the words on the lines. *Clue: the last letter of each word is the first letter of the next word.*

QUAILAWILDERNESSINAISRAEL

ISTENEEDSINNEDESERTIRING

RUMBLINGODAILYEARAIN

_ _ _ _ _, _ _ _, _ _ _ _ _ _ _ _ _ _,

_ _ _ _ _, _ _ _ _ _ _, _ _ _ _ _ _,

_ _ _ _ _, _ _ _ _ _ _, _ _ _ _ _ _,

_ _ _ _ _ _ _, _ _ _ _ _ _ _ _,

_ _ _, _ _ _ _ _, _ _ _ _, _ _ _ _

16

7. Jonathan and David

Jonathan and David are best friends. Starting at different places, they are going to meet at a rock in the center of a field. Can you help each of them find the right path?

8. Solomon's Temple

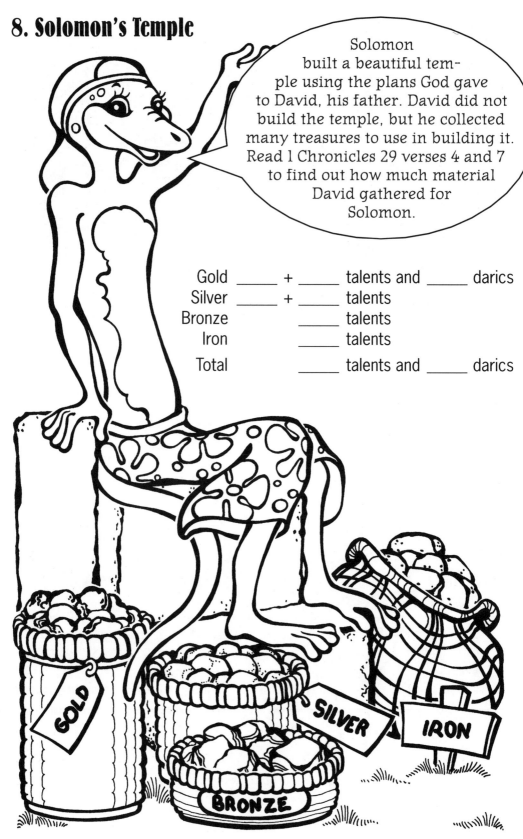

Solomon built a beautiful temple using the plans God gave to David, his father. David did not build the temple, but he collected many treasures to use in building it. Read 1 Chronicles 29 verses 4 and 7 to find out how much material David gathered for Solomon.

Gold _____ + _____ talents and _____ darics
Silver _____ + _____ talents
Bronze _____ talents
Iron _____ talents
Total _____ talents and _____ darics

The roof was made of _____ planks (v. 9). The inside walls were made of _____ boards. The floor of the temple was made of _____ (v. 15). The inside of the inner sanctuary was lined in _____. There were ____ chains across the front (vv. 19–22). In the inner sanctuary there were two _____ of _____ wood (v. 23) overlaid with _____(v. 28). The doors to the inner sanctuary were made of _____ wood, carved with _____, _____ _____, and open _____ (vv. 34–35).

9. Another Temple

Solomon's beautiful temple was destroyed by Judah's enemies. Years later Ezra went back to Jerusalem to rebuild the temple. Unscramble the letters to discover what Ezra took with him and how many of each. (The answers are found in Ezra 1:9–10 and 2:64–66.)

	Things Ezra took	How many?
DLGO SSDHIE	_____	_____
VRLESI SHSEDI	_____	_____
VERLIS SPNA	_____	_____
OGDL WLOBS	_____	_____
REVISL SLOBW	_____	_____

	People that went along	How many?
TERAVSNS	_____	_____
GERNISS	_____	_____
LHEOW PCNOMYA	_____	_____

	Animals that carried everything	How many?
RESOSH	_____	_____
LEMUS	_____	_____
SEMACL	_____	_____
NODYSEK	_____	_____

10. Job's Riches

Job, a very rich man, had many animals. In Job 1:3 there is a list of the animals he owned. Count them to see how rich he was.

sheep _____
camels _____
yoke of oxen _____
donkeys _____

total _____

After Job lost all his animals and had many other troubles, God blessed Job because he believed God's promises. In the last chapter of Job (verse 12) there is another list of all the animals Job owned. Count them now.

sheep _____
camels _____
yoke of oxen _____
donkeys _____

total _____

See how God blessed Job? He gave him twice as many animals as he had in the beginning!

22

11. A Great God

$$\overline{11}\ \overline{8}\ \overline{11}\ \overline{12}\ \overline{3}\ '\quad \overline{11}\ \overline{15}\ \overline{12}\ \overline{8}\ \overline{11}\ \overline{12}\ \overline{3}\ '$$

$$\overline{5}\ \overline{11}\ \overline{16}\quad \overline{9}\ \overline{1}\ \overline{7}\ \overline{4}\ \overline{13}\ \overline{14}\ \overline{6}\ \overline{2}$$

$$\overline{6}\ \overline{13}\quad \overline{17}\ \overline{11}\ \overline{15}\ \overline{12}\quad \overline{10}\ \overline{1}\ \overline{9}\ \overline{4}$$

$$\overline{6}\ \overline{10}\quad \overline{1}\ \overline{8}\ \overline{8}\quad \overline{14}\ \overline{5}\ \overline{4}\quad \overline{4}\ \overline{1}\ \overline{12}\ \overline{14}\ \overline{5}\ !$$

David sang a song of praise to God in Psalm 8. The first part of the first verse is set in code. Use the key to unscramble it.

A	C	D	E	H	I
1	2	3	4	5	6

J	L	M	N	O	R
7	8	9	10	11	12

S	T	U	W	Y
13	14	15	16	17

23

12. Praise God!

This verse describes something all of God's children should do every day. Find the words of the text hidden in the puzzle below. The words may be hidden up, down, backward, forward, and diagonally.

I will praise you, O LORD, with all my heart; I will tell of all your wonders.

Psalm 9:1

13. A Message from the Sun

The person who wrote Psalm 19 was praising God for his wonderful creation. There is a circle of letters surrounding the sun above. Start at the arrow and record the message on the lines below. Some of the letters—B, I, J, and Z—are extra, so you should not use them.

___ ___ ___ ___ ___ ___ ___ ___ ___ ___ ___ ___ ___ ___ ___ ___ ___ ___ ___

___ ___ ___ ___ ___ ___ ___ ___ ___ ___ ___ (Psalm 19:1).

14. A Coded Message

N	U	R	K
14	1	9	13

S	O	L
11	2	8

V	H	P	T	Y
16	7	17	6	20

M	I	D	A	G
19	3	10	5	12

F	E
18	4

B
15

Use the code above to discover the message on the next page. If you need help, find Psalm 95 and read verses 3–5.

6 7 4 8 2 9 10 3 11 6 7 4

12 9 4 5 6 12 2 10' 6 7 4 12 9 4 5 6

13 3 14 12 5 15 2 16 4 5 8 8 12 2 10 11.

3 14 7 3 11 7 5 14 10 5 9 4 6 7 4

10 4 17 6 7 11 2 18 6 7 4 4 5 9 6 7'

5 14 10 6 7 4 19 2 1 14 6 5 3 14

17 4 5 13 11 15 4 8 2 14 12 6 2 7 3 19.

6 7 4 11 4 5 3 11 7 3 11' 18 2 9

7 4 19 5 10 4 3 6' 5 14 10 7 3 11

7 5 14 10 11 18 2 9 19 4 10 6 7 4

10 9 20 8 5 14 10.

27

15. God's World

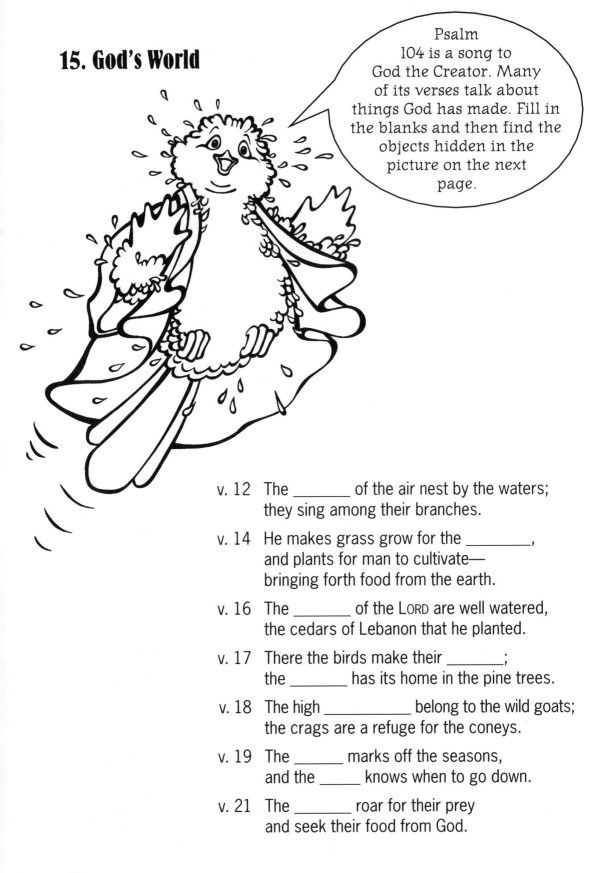

Psalm 104 is a song to God the Creator. Many of its verses talk about things God has made. Fill in the blanks and then find the objects hidden in the picture on the next page.

v. 12 The _____ of the air nest by the waters;
they sing among their branches.

v. 14 He makes grass grow for the _____,
and plants for man to cultivate—
bringing forth food from the earth.

v. 16 The _____ of the LORD are well watered,
the cedars of Lebanon that he planted.

v. 17 There the birds make their _____;
the _____ has its home in the pine trees.

v. 18 The high _____ belong to the wild goats;
the crags are a refuge for the coneys.

v. 19 The _____ marks off the seasons,
and the _____ knows when to go down.

v. 21 The _____ roar for their prey
and seek their food from God.

16. Plagues on Egypt

Psalm 105 talks about the ten plagues God sent before the Israelites left Egypt. Read especially verses 29–34 to discover more about the plagues. Fill in the blanks below and then find the objects hidden in the drawing on the next page.

v. 29 He turned their waters into blood, causing their _____ to die.

v. 30 Their land teemed with _____, which went up into the bedrooms of their rulers.

v. 31 He spoke, and there came swarms of _____, and gnats throughout their country.

v. 32 He turned their rain into hail, with _____ throughout their land.

v. 34 He spoke, and the locusts came, _____ without number.

17. Reading the Hebrew Way

If you were a Hebrew boy or girl, you would learn the Hebrew alphabet and you would learn to read from the right to the left—this way:

E-S-I-A-R-P

But the Hebrew alphabet doesn't have any vowels—A, E, I, O, and U. When the letters A, E, and I are dropped from the word *praise,* and it is read from right to left, it looks like this:

S-R-P

See if you can read some familiar texts if the words have no vowels and they are read from right to left. Write the text on the lines below.

D-R-L   H-T   S-R-P (Psalm 150:1)

_____

D-R-H-P-H-S   Y-M   S   D-R-L   H-T (Psalm 23:1)

_____

H-T-R   H-T   D-N   S-N-V-H   H-T   D-T-R-C   D-G   G-N-N-N-G-B   H-T   N (Genesis 1:1)

32

18. A Wicked Person

goes about with a corrupt _____

winks with his _____

signals with his _____

plots evil with deceit in his _____

motions with his _____

In Proverbs 6:12–14, Solomon describes a wicked person. Match the picture in column two with the correct words in column one.

19. Good Advice

In the Book of Proverbs, Solomon gives many instructions. In each box are letters that make up words in some of those instructions. Unscramble the letters and write each correct word on the right line to see what Solomon says. If you need help, check the verses from Proverbs that are listed by each statement.

HTE   ORLD

_____   _____   (2:6).
IGEVS   SWIODM

EKPE   YROU   OTFO

_____   _____   (4:27).
OFMR   VELI

OD   ONT   EB   IWES

_____   _____   _____   _____   (3:7).
NI   OUYR   ONW   EESY

OD ONT ETS FTOO

NO HTE PTHA

FO TEH CWDIKE (4:14).

AYLZ NHASD AMEK A

AMN OPRO' UBT

IDILETGN DAHNS

RBNGI AWEHTL (10:4).

EB UESR FO ITHS:

HET CWEIKD LWIL OTN

OG NPIUNHSEUD (11:21).

20. Solomon Says

_____ that rush into evil

haughty (proud) _____

a lying _____

_____ that shed innocent blood

a _____ that devises wicked schemes

a _____ who stirs up dissension (trouble)

In Proverbs 6:16–19, Solomon lists things that God hates. Fill in the blanks; then draw a line to the correct picture in column two.

21. Matching Time

Ecclesiastes 3 says there is a time for everything. Match the event or action in the first column with the correct event or action from the second column. The answers are found in Ecclesiastes 3:2–8.

A time to   **and**   **a time to**

___ 1. be born   a. speak
___ 2. plant   b. throw away
___ 3. kill   c. gather stones
___ 4. tear down   d. laugh
___ 5. weep   e. heal
___ 6. mourn   f. die
___ 7. scatter stones   g. make peace
___ 8. search   h. uproot
___ 9. keep   i. hate
___ 10. tear   j. build
___ 11. be silent   k. mend
___ 12. love   l. dance
___ 13. make war   m. give up

22. What's an Idol?

KLIE A WCSAROERC
_____ _ _____

NI A NMELO CPTHA'
__ _ _____ _____,

RTHEI DLSOI
_____ _____

NNTOAC KPSAE
_____ _____.

There are many kinds of
idols. God told Jeremiah what an
idol was like and then Jeremiah told
the Israelites. Unscramble the words
above and then draw a picture that
matches Jeremiah's description.
(You can read the description
in Jeremiah 10:5.)

23. A Wonderful Promise

In Zephaniah 3:17 there is a wonderful promise from God. Use the code to read the promise below.

Code:

1	3	5	7	9	11	13	15	17	19	21	23	25
A	B	C	D	E	F	G	H	I	J	K	L	M

27	29	31	33	35	37	39	41	43	45	47	49	51
N	O	P	Q	R	S	T	U	V	W	X	Y	Z

39 15 9   23 29 35 7   49 29 41 35

13 29 7   17 37 45 17 39 15

49 29 41 , 15 9 17 37

25 17 13 15 39 49   39 29   37 1 43 9

40

24. A Message for Joseph

To find out what an angel told Joseph, move across the squares twice, using only the letters in the odd-numbered columns the first time and only the letters in the even-numbered columns the second time. Write the message on the lines below the wall.

1	2	3	4	5	6	7	8	9	10
S	E	H	J	E	E	W	S	I	U
L	S	L	B	G	E	I	C	V	A
E	U	B	S	I	E	R	H	T	E
H	W	T	I	O	L	A	L	S	S
O	A	N	V	A	E	N	H	D	I
Y	S	O	P	U	E	A	O	R	P
E	L	T	E	O	F	G	R	I	O
V	M	E	T	H	H	I	E	M	I
T	R	H	S	E	I	N	N	A	S
M									

___ _____ ____ _____

__ _ ____, ___ ___ ___

__ _____ ___ ___ ____

_____, _____ __ ____

____ ___ _____

_____ _____ _____ (Matthew 1:21).

42

26. Christmas Words

ARTS   _ _ A _

ARIOVS   _ A _ _ _ _

ALTEBS   _ _ A _ _ _

AENGLS   A _ _ _ _ _

ABBY   _ A _ _

ANEGMR   _ A _ _ _ _

ARYM   _ A _ _

Many words used in the Christmas story have an A in them. Some of those words are scrambled above. Unscramble them and fill in the puzzle blanks.

44

27. A Christmas Flower

Color the R spaces red, the G spaces green, and the Y spaces yellow. Then color the flowerpot and fill in the background with your favorite colors.

28. The Angels' Song

To unscramble the angels' song, move across the squares twice, using only the letters in the odd-numbered columns the first time and only the letters in the even-numbered columns the second time. Write the message on the lines below the wall.

1	2	3	4	5	6	7	8	9	10
G	H	L	P	O	E	R	A	Y	C
T	E	O	T	G	O	O	M	D	E
I	N	N	O	T	N	H	W	E	H
H	O	I	M	G	H	H	I	E	S
S	F	T	A	A	V	N	O	D	R
O	R	N	E	E	S	A	T	R	S
T									

_____ __ ___ __ ___

_____, ___ __ _____

_____ __ ___ __ ____

___ _____ _____ (Luke 2:14).

46

29. The Lost Shepherd

Start

Marcus got lost on his way to Bethlehem to see the baby Jesus. Can you help him find his way?

30. Forty-two Generations

J

_____

_____

_____

_____

_____

_____

_____

_____

_____

A

_____

_____

_____

_____

_____

_____

_____

_____

```
K U P Q Z C G Q U W I J Z Q Z
Z P J O T H A M F J I E I J C
C R X N W E A Y R E Y H Z P T
N H A I N O C E T O J O Q I L
G L M A H A Z G A S O R X Z M
B I C W L Q E Y I E P A K I Z
J U D A H J C N B P H M A K A
V I U B J G Q O V H A A M E M
G I I I G H Q M X A T H A S M
X F B J H I O A C T J R S S I
M X A A I H W C A J J B U E N
R O U H H M B Q J J C A S J A
O H A I M Z R O O D G V E F D
Z M H T H Z I S C G C Z J X A
A S A O Z T S B B I I T Z Z B
```

31. Generations

How many words having three or more letters can you make from the letters in the word *generations*?

GENERATIONS

Super Word Finder

Great Word Finder

Good Word Finder

Word Champion

50

32. A String of Fish

Instead of swallowing a hook, each of these fish swallowed a word. Match the fish below with the fish on Jake's stringer to put the words in order. Check Matthew 19:17 if you need help.

LIFE

OBEY

IF

ENTER

THE

TO

YOU

WANT

COMMANDMENTS

51

33. Miracles of Jesus

Matthew, Mark, Luke, and John wrote about many miracles Jesus performed. Use the Scripture references listed below to discover what Jesus said and did. Then color the objects in the drawing on the next page.

John 4:50   "You may go. Your ___ will live."

Luke 5:24   "Get up, take your ___ and go home."

Mark 6:39   Then Jesus directed them to have all the _____ sit down in groups on the green _____.

John 9:6   He spit on the ground, made some mud with the saliva, and put it on the man's _____.

John 21:6   "Throw your ___ on the right side of the ____."

Matthew 17:27   "Take the first ___ you catch; open its _____ and you will find a four-drachma ____."

John 2:7   "Fill the ____ with water."

34. Stories Jesus Told

When Jesus tried to teach the people about God and his kingdom, he often used stories. Use the Scripture references listed below to find some of the simple things Jesus talked about in his stories. Then look for those things in the drawing on the next page.

Matthew 13:45–46   valuable _____

Matthew 18:12–14   lost _____

Luke 15:8–10   lost _____

Mark 2:21   new cloth on an old _____

Luke 15:11–32   lost ___

Matthew 13:44   hidden _____

Matthew 25:31–46   sheep and _____

Luke 11:33   ____ under a ____

Matthew 13:47–50   fishing ___

35. The Disciples

The Bible tells us about twelve men who followed Jesus. We call these men *disciples*. Their names fit in the stack-a-word grid below. If you need some help, look in Matthew 10:2–4.

36. Letter Wheels

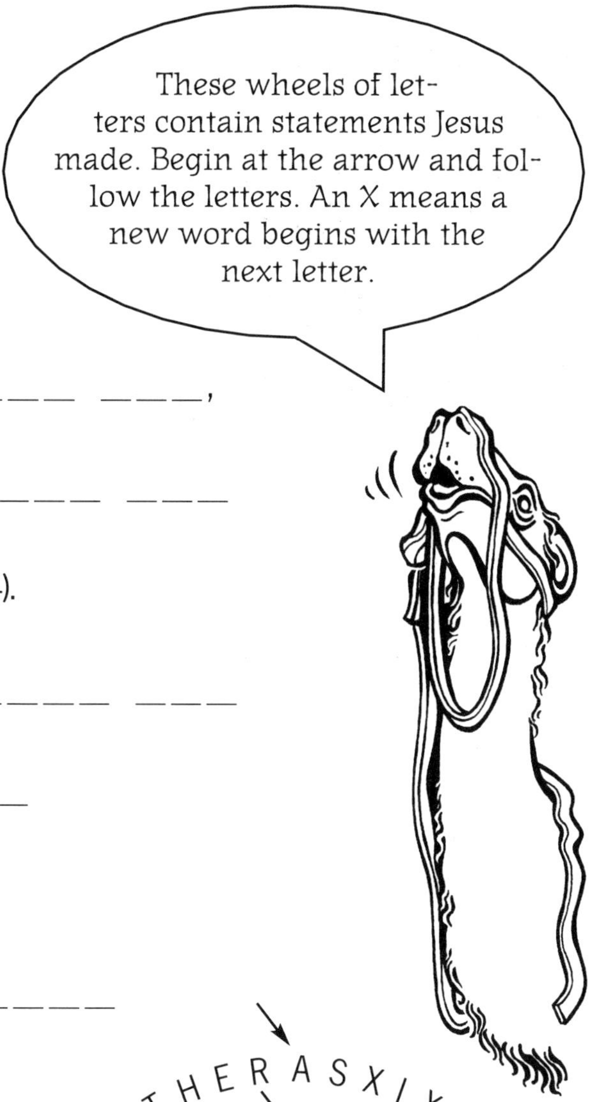

These wheels of letters contain statements Jesus made. Begin at the arrow and follow the letters. An X means a new word begins with the next letter.

"__ _ ____ _____ ___,

__ ___ ____ ____ ___

_______" (John 13:34).

"_ ____ ____ ____ ___

____ ___ __ __

____ __" (John 14:3).

"_ ___ ___ ______

___ ___" (John 10:30).

ASXIXHAVEXLOVEDXYOUXSOXYOUXMUSTXLOVEXONEXANOTHER
IXWILLXCOMEXBACKXANDXTAKEXYOUXTOXBEXWITHXME
IXANDXTHEXFATHERXAREXONE

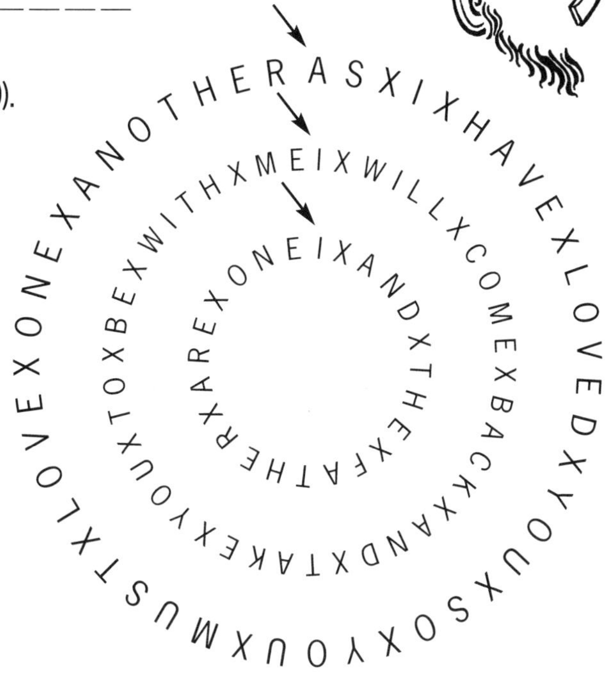

37. More Miracles

Tobi was going to tell you about some of the miracles Jesus did. But Tobi stumbled and scrambled the letters. Use the Scripture references if you need help unscrambling Jesus' words.

__ __ __ __ __ __ __! Mark 1:41
E B   L N E A C

__ __ __' __ __ __ __ __ __ __ __
N S O   R O U Y   S S N I

__ __ __ __ __ __ __ __ __ __. Mark 2:5
E R A   R G O I E N F V

__ __ __ __ __ __ __!
E B   T U Q I E

__ __ __ __ __ __ __ __ __ __ __ __! Mark 1:25
O E M C   T O U   F O   M I H

__ __ __ __ __ __ __ __ __ __
T T R C S E H   T O U

__ __ __ __ __ __ __ __. Mark 3:5
Y R O U   N D A H

_____! Mark 4:3
L N S T I E

38. Who's in the Tree?

Someone climbed this tree to see Jesus. Do you know who it is? Connect the dots and color the picture. Then write the person's name on the blank line at the bottom of the page.

39. A Needle's Eye

Jesus said it would be easier for this animal to go through the eye of a needle (that's the little slit at the top) than for a rich man to enter the kingdom of heaven. Connect the dots to complete the animal Jesus used in this example.

40. Beatitudes

Read chapter five of Matthew and match those who are blessed with their blessing. Draw a line from the first column to the blessing in the second column.

Blessed are	**for they (theirs is)**
poor in spirit	will be filled
persecuted because of righteousness	the kingdom of heaven
merciful	will be called sons of God
meek	the kingdom of heaven
pure in heart	will inherit the earth
those who hunger and thirst for righteousness	will be comforted
those who mourn	will be shown mercy
peacemakers	will see God

41. Another String of Fish

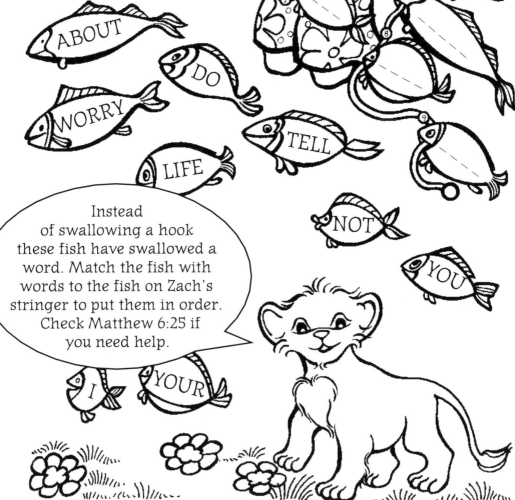

Instead of swallowing a hook these fish have swallowed a word. Match the fish with words to the fish on Zach's stringer to put them in order. Check Matthew 6:25 if you need help.

ABOUT

DO

WORRY

TELL

LIFE

NOT

YOU

I

YOUR

42. Jesus Cares for All Creatures

Jesus cares for all creatures, even small ones. Connect the dots and color the picture below of some of God's precious creatures.

43. Jesus and Animals

Jesus talked about animals several times while he was on earth. Look up the Scripture references to find the name of each animal and then find the animal in the drawing on the next page.

Matthew 8:20   _____ have holes and _____ of the air have nests.

Matthew 15:26   It is not right to take the children's bread and toss it to their _____.

Luke 11:12   Or if he asks for an egg, will you give him a _____?

Mark 10:25   It is easier for a _____ to go through the eye of a needle than for a rich man to enter the kingdom of God.

Matthew 12:40   Jonah was three days and three nights in the belly of a huge _____.

Luke 22:34   Before the _____ crows today, you will deny three times that you know me.

Matthew 10:16   I am sending you out like _____ among _____. Therefore be as shrewd as _____ and as innocent as _____.

44. Cities Jesus Visited

Unscramble the names of some of the cities Jesus visited while he was on earth. Then use a map in the back of a Bible to help you put the names of the cities in the correct location on the next page.

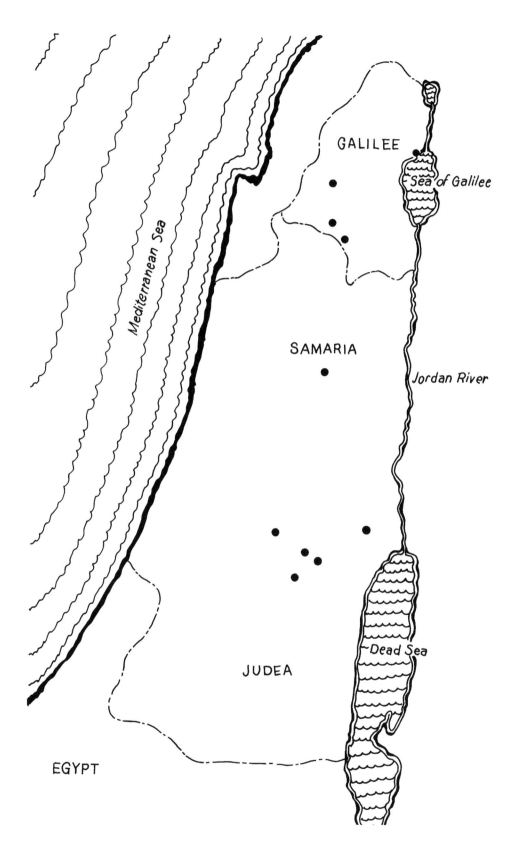

GALILEE

Sea of Galilee

Mediterranean Sea

SAMARIA

Jordan River

Dead Sea

JUDEA

EGYPT

45. Smoke Signals

Can you read the messages in the smoke signal above? Follow the smoke until you reach a letter and then write the letter in one of the squares above the smoke.

46. Mary and Martha's House

Start

Little Zeke wants to visit his friends Mary and Martha who live in Bethany. He can't remember how to get there though. Will you help him find his way?

47. Missing Lines

The signmaker has some messages to put on some signs. But he forgot to put all the lines in the letters. Can you help him?

48. Hidden Treasure

Jesus talked about a man who hid a valuable treasure in a field. Follow the maze to find it.

Start

49. Jerusalem

The most famous city mentioned in the Bible is Jerusalem. David lived in Jerusalem, and Jesus visited Jerusalem. People live in Jerusalem today too. How many words of three or more letters can you make from the letters in *Jerusalem*? Can you find a six-letter word?

JERUSALEM

_____ _____ _____ _____

_____ _____ _____ _____

_____ _____ _____ _____

_____ _____ _____ _____

_____ _____ _____ _____

_____ _____ _____ _____

_____ _____ Super Word Finder _____

_____ _____ _____ _____

_____ _____ _____ _____

_____ Great Word Finder _____ _____

_____ _____ _____ _____

_____ _____ _____ _____

Good Word Finder _____ _____ Word Champion

50. More Smoke Signals

Can you read the smoke signal above? Follow the smoke up from the fire to a letter and write the letter in one of the squares above the smoke.

51. An Easter Flower

Color the G spaces green, the Y spaces yellow, the W spaces white, and the P spaces purple. Then fill in the background with your favorite colors.

74

52. Easter Words

Many words in the Easter story have an E in them. Use the key below to fill in the blanks.

$\overline{1}\ \overline{15}\ \overline{14}\ \overline{2}\ \overline{11}$

$\overline{10}\ \overline{6}\ \overline{4}\ \overline{15}\ \overline{2}$

$\overline{10}\ \overline{4}\ \overline{11}\ \overline{8}\ \overline{3}\ \overline{2}\ \overline{7}\ \overline{10}$

$\overline{17}\ \overline{2}\ \overline{10}\ \overline{5}\ \overline{10}$

$\overline{2}\ \overline{1}\ \overline{10}\ \overline{6}\ \overline{2}\ \overline{7}$

$\overline{14}\ \overline{1}\ \overline{7}\ \overline{8}\ \overline{2}\ \overline{15}$

$\overline{2}\ \overline{18}\ \overline{9}\ \overline{6}\ \overline{12}\ \ \ \overline{6}\ \overline{4}\ \overline{18}\ \overline{13}$

Key:

$\dfrac{A}{1}\quad \dfrac{B}{13}\quad \dfrac{D}{8}\quad \dfrac{E}{2}\quad \dfrac{G}{14}\quad \dfrac{I}{3}\quad \dfrac{J}{17}\quad \dfrac{L}{11}\quad \dfrac{M}{18}\quad \dfrac{N}{15}\quad \dfrac{O}{4}\quad \dfrac{P}{9}\quad \dfrac{R}{7}\quad \dfrac{S}{10}\quad \dfrac{T}{6}\quad \dfrac{U}{5}\quad \dfrac{Y}{12}$

54. Ascension

JESUS SAT DOWN
AT THE RIGHT HAND
OF THE FATHER
IN HEAVEN.

When Jesus went back to heaven he did something. The words describing his action fit in the stack-a-word grid. See if you can fill the grid.

55. An Oil Lamp

56. Peter's Sermon

When Peter preached his sermon on Pentecost, this is one of the things he said:

All of the words will fit into the puzzle below. Can you fill the grid?

Everyone who calls on the name of the Lord will be saved (Acts 2:21).

57. A Confused Soldier

Start

TO DAMASCUS →

One of the soldiers who was going to help Saul find Christians in Damascus overslept, so Saul left without him. Now the soldier needs to find his own way there. He needs help because something strange is happening. Read more about it in Acts 9.

58. An Important Question

The Philippian jailer asked Paul and Silas, "What must I do to be saved?" They gave him a good answer. Can you decode it? If you need help, see Acts 16:31.

O	I	V	G	B	J	E	X	K	M	F	Q	A
A	B	C	D	E	F	G	H	I	J	K	L	M

R	S	Z	W	L	D	P	Y	H	T	C	N	U
N	O	P	Q	R	S	T	U	V	W	X	Y	Z

I B Q K B H B

K R P X B Q S L G M B D Y D'

O R G N S Y T K Q Q I B D O H B G.

59. A Promise

In 1 Corinthians 15:21–22 Paul gives us a wonderful promise.

For since death came through a man, the resurrection of the dead comes also through a man. For as in Adam all die, so in Christ all will be made alive.

Find the words of this promise in the word search puzzle. If a word is in the promise two times, it is hidden only once in the puzzle. Words are hidden up, down, backward, forward, and diagonally.

```
B L T H R O U G H
P W D I E P A T H
A I T R S A H O T
O L M H U O T H E
L D A C R S A O C
O M B D R L E A N
T E D A E A D O I
S A A S C O M E S
I N M T T O P E S
R N S L I V A I N
H N O F O R A I N
C O R D N A M E N
```

60. A Parting Blessing

Paul closed many of his letters in a special way, often called a benediction. One benediction has become so well known that it is called the Apostolic Benediction. It is found in 2 Corinthians 13:14.

May the grace of the Lord Jesus Christ, and the love of God, and the fellowship of the Holy Spirit be with you all.

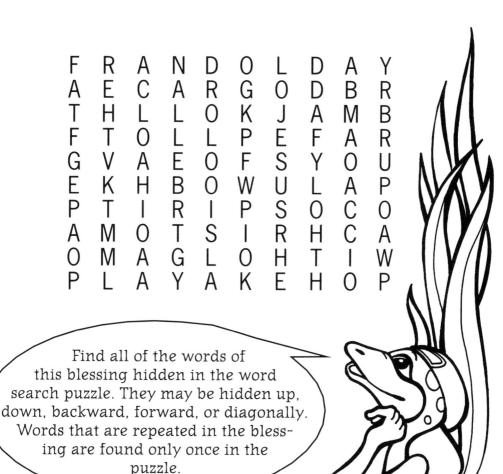

```
F  R  A  N  D  O  L  D  A  Y
A  E  C  A  R  G  O  D  B  R
T  H  L  L  O  K  J  A  M  B
F  T  O  L  L  P  E  F  A  R
G  V  A  E  O  F  S  Y  O  U
E  K  H  B  O  W  U  L  A  P
P  T  I  R  I  P  S  O  C  O
A  M  O  T  S  I  R  H  C  A
O  M  A  G  L  O  H  T  I  W
P  L  A  Y  A  K  E  H  O  P
```

Find all of the words of this blessing hidden in the word search puzzle. They may be hidden up, down, backward, forward, or diagonally. Words that are repeated in the blessing are found only once in the puzzle.

61. Places Paul Visited

MEARLUJSE _ _ _ _ _ _ _ _ _   RAAAEESC _ _ _ _ _ _ _ _

SAPTOM _ _ _ _ _ _   TANHIOC _ _ _ _ _ _ _

RATSSU _ _ _ _ _ _   YRSTLA _ _ _ _ _ _

GEPRA _ _ _ _ _   PHEEUSS _ _ _ _ _ _ _

NASYMR _ _ _ _ _ _   OTSRA _ _ _ _ _

NHTEAS _ _ _ _ _ _   NRTHCIO _ _ _ _ _ _ _

EEARB _ _ _ _ _

Unscramble the names of the places Paul visited on his first two missionary journeys. Then use the map in the back of your Bible to help you put the names of the cities in the correct locations on the map on the next page.

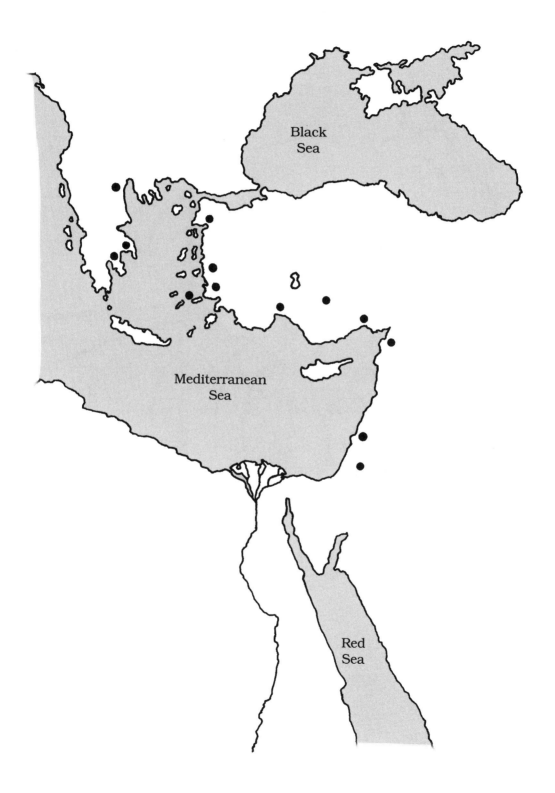

Black
Sea

Mediterranean
Sea

Red
Sea

85

62. Heroes of Faith

In Hebrews 11 there is a roll call of Old Testament heroes of faith. First, unscramble the names below and then find them hidden in the word search on the next page.

NGDIOE _ _ _ _ _ _

ARABH _ _ _ _ _

NOASSM _ _ _ _ _ _

OESJPH _ _ _ _ _ _

SMSOE _ _ _ _ _

EALB _ _ _ _

AIDDV _ _ _ _ _

HSAAR _ _ _ _ _

HPTHHAEJ _ _ _ _ _ _ _ _

BHAAMAR _ _ _ _ _ _ _

AHNO _ _ _ _

CHENO _ _ _ _ _

CAISA _ _ _ _ _

ACJBO _ _ _ _ _

KAABR _ _ _ _ _

LAUSME _ _ _ _ _ _

```
E H A H T H P E J O
A B L E U M A S K E
C G I D E O N A L T
M O E I S A R R E S
P D A V O A B A O A
R A H A B R A H A M
E B C D O M O S E S
H E O L C A A S I O
T L N O A P H A O N
S I E T J O S E P H
```

63. Benediction

The word *benediction* means last words or blessing. Often we hear a benediction just before we leave church. How many words of three or more letters can you make from the letters in *benediction*?

BENEDICTION

_____ _____ _____ _____

_____ _____ _____ _____

_____ _____ _____ _____

_____ _____ _____ _____

_____   _____

_____ _____ Super Word Finder _____

_____ _____ _____ _____

_____ _____ _____ _____

_____ Great Word Finder _____ _____

_____ _____ _____ _____

_____ _____ _____ _____

Good Word Finder _____ _____ Word Champion

64. Two Promises

There are two special promises in Hebrews 13:5–6. Try to discover what they are without looking in your Bible. Start at the arrow and work around each circle, using all of the letters except Z, Q, X, and C.

QBQEZXAQFZRXAQIQD ZXTHQEZXLQOZXRQDZIXSQMZXYQHELQZPXERZIQWIZXLZLQNXOZT

___ ____ __ __ _____;

_ ____ ___ __ _____.

NEQVXECRZWQILLCIZXQLQEAVZXECYQYOXUZNQEVVZECRZWQILXCIZQFORQXSZAQKQEXYCOZUC

_____ ____ _ _____ ___;

_____ ____ _ _____ ___.

89

65. Preaching

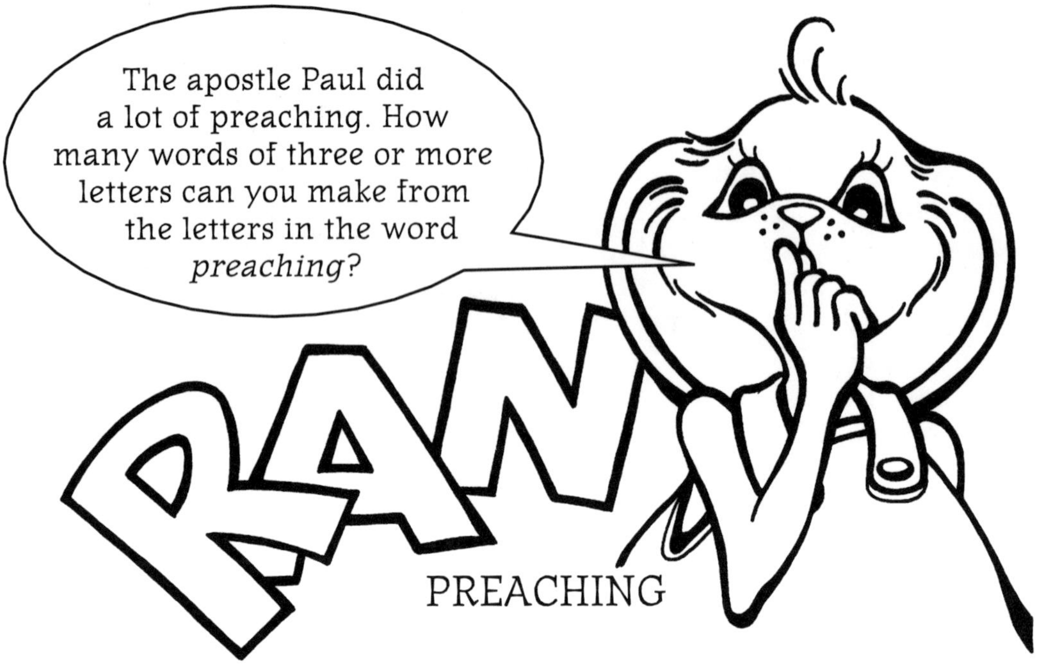

The apostle Paul did a lot of preaching. How many words of three or more letters can you make from the letters in the word *preaching*?

PREACHING

Super Word Finder

Great Word Finder

Good Word Finder

Word Champion

66. James Says

James the brother of Jesus wrote one of the books in the New Testament. In the first chapter of his book, James gives some easy-to-remember rules. Put the words of verse 22 in the grid.

Do not merely listen to the word, and so deceive yourselves. Do what it says.

67. Reading the Hebrew Way

If you were a Hebrew boy or girl, you would learn the Hebrew alphabet and you would learn to read from the right to the left—this way:

E-S-I-A-R-P

But the Hebrew alphabet doesn't have any vowels—A, E, I, O, and U. When the letters A, E, and I are dropped from the word *praise,* and it is read from right to left, it looks like this:

S-R-P

See if you can read some familiar texts if the words have no vowels and they are read from right to left. Write the text on the lines below.

?S T-S-N-G B N-C H-W S R-F S D-G F (Romans 8:31)

_____

V-L S D-G (1 John 4:16)

_____

S-D-N-M-M-C S-H Y-B T D-G R-F V-L S S-H-T (1 John 5:3)

_____

68. Word Search

Some of the words hidden in the puzzle below are from Revelation 5:11–12. Find the words hidden up, down, backward, forward, and diagonally.

BLESSING	HONOR	POWER	SLAIN
CROSS	JESUS	RECEIVE	STRENGTH
GLORY	LAMB	REVELATION	VOICE
GOD	LOUD	RICHES	WISDOM

```
R E W O P H R E A N
I E C I O V W A T O
C S V J E S U S E I
H R T E B M A S V T
E O O R L E T L I A
S N L S E A L A E L
G O U T S N T I C E
T H D P S U G N E V
M O G S I W E T R E
A N E S N I I H R R
Y R L L G O D L Y O
```

69. Revelation

The last book in the Bible is called Revelation. John wrote it and tried to tell us what God allowed him to see about future events. How many three-letter (or more) words can you make from the letters in the word *revelation*?

REVELATION

_____   _____   _____   _____

_____   _____   _____   _____

_____   _____   _____   _____

_____   _____   _____   _____

_____   _____   _____   _____

Super Word Finder

_____   _____   _____   _____

_____   _____   _____   _____

_____   _____   _____   _____

Great Word Finder

_____   _____   _____   _____

_____   _____   _____   _____

Good Word Finder   _____   _____   Word Champion

Miscellaneous
Activities

70. Bible Bookmark

Cut out and color both sides of these bookmarks. Then paste the two sides of each together back-to-back. You can use it to help you find the books of the Bible.

Front

BOOKS OF THE OLD TESTAMENT

Genesis	Ecclesiastes
Exodus	Song of Songs
Leviticus	Isaiah
Numbers	Jeremiah
Deuteronomy	Lamentations
Joshua	Ezekiel
Judges	Daniel
Ruth	Hosea
1 Samuel	Joel
2 Samuel	Amos
1 Kings	Obadiah
2 Kings	Jonah
1 Chronicles	Micah
2 Chronicles	Nahum
Ezra	Habakkuk
Nehemiah	Zephaniah
Esther	Haggai
Job	Zechariah
Psalms	Malachi
Proverbs	

_____
Your Name

God Loves Me

Back

Front   Back

BOOKS OF THE
NEW TESTAMENT

Matthew	1 Timothy
Mark	2 Timothy
Luke	Titus
John	Philemon
Acts	Hebrews
Romans	James
1 Corinthians	1 Peter
2 Corinthians	2 Peter
Galatians	1 John
Ephesians	2 John
Philippians	3 John
Colossians	Jude
1 Thessalonians	Revelation
2 Thessalonians	

_____

Your Name

I Love God

71. Facts about the Bible

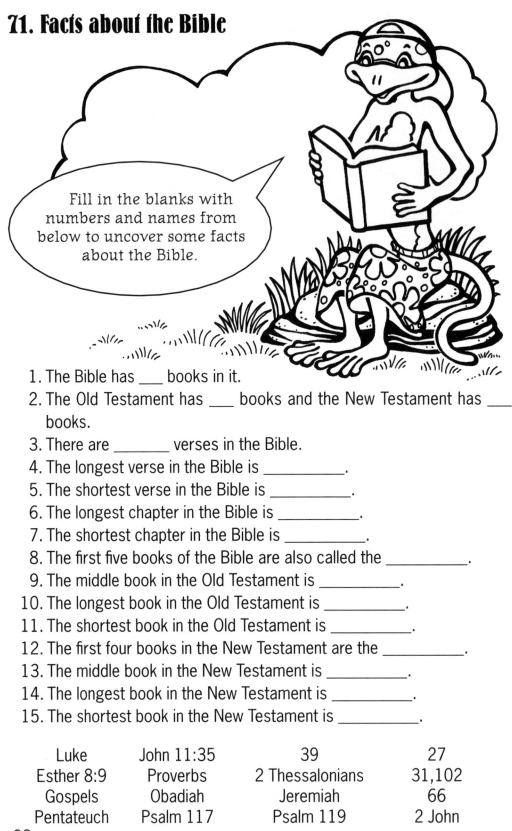

Fill in the blanks with numbers and names from below to uncover some facts about the Bible.

1. The Bible has ___ books in it.
2. The Old Testament has ___ books and the New Testament has ___ books.
3. There are _____ verses in the Bible.
4. The longest verse in the Bible is _____.
5. The shortest verse in the Bible is _____.
6. The longest chapter in the Bible is _____.
7. The shortest chapter in the Bible is _____.
8. The first five books of the Bible are also called the _____.
9. The middle book in the Old Testament is _____.
10. The longest book in the Old Testament is _____.
11. The shortest book in the Old Testament is _____.
12. The first four books in the New Testament are the _____.
13. The middle book in the New Testament is _____.
14. The longest book in the New Testament is _____.
15. The shortest book in the New Testament is _____.

Luke	John 11:35	39	27
Esther 8:9	Proverbs	2 Thessalonians	31,102
Gospels	Obadiah	Jeremiah	66
Pentateuch	Psalm 117	Psalm 119	2 John

72. Trumpets

Fill in the stack-a-word grid by using the Scripture references listed for each clue.

1. _____ placed trumpets and empty jars in the hands of all the men (Judges 7:15–16).

2. Sound the trumpet at the new _____ (Psalm 81:3).

3. _____ God with the sounding of the trumpet (Psalm 150:3).

4. Raise your _____ like a trumpet (Isaiah 58:1).

5. Blow the trumpet in Zion; sound the _____ on my holy hill (Joel 2:1).

6. The sovereign _____ will sound the trumpet (Zechariah 9:14).

7. With the trumpet call of God . . . the _____ in Christ will rise (1 Thessalonians 4:16).

8. I _____ behind me a loud voice like a trumpet (Revelation 1:10).

9. The sixth _____ had a trumpet (Revelation 9:14).

10. On the morning of the third day there was . . . a loud trumpet _____ (Exodus 19:16).

73. Counting Stars

There are lots of stars on this page. If you circle the correct number of stars to answer each question, there should be just one star left uncircled.

1. How old was Jesus when he went to the temple? (Luke 2:42) _____

2. How many stones did David pick up from the stream to use in his slingshot? (1 Samuel 17:40) _____

3. How many spies did Rahab hide? (Joshua 2:4) _____

4. How many of Daniel's friends were thrown into the fiery furnace? (Daniel 3:19–20) _____

5. How many sons did the priest Eli have? (1 Samuel 2:34) _____

6. How many time did Peter deny Jesus? (John 18:17–27) _____

7. How many books of the Bible have only one chapter? _____

8. How many brothers did King David have? (1 Samuel 17:12) _____

75. Bible Animals

Many animals are named in the Bible. Here are a few of them, but their names are scrambled. Unscramble the names and find all the animals on the next page.

sape	_____	2 Chronicles 9:21
bbrati	_____	Leviticus 11:6
gdo	_____	Ecclesiastes 9:4
sxefo	_____	Song of Songs 2:15
mclea	_____	Mark 10:25
kjaalc	_____	Micah 1:8
rhrso	_____	Exodus 15:21
xo	_____	Proverbs 7:22
blma	_____	Leviticus 12:6
gsip	_____	Mark 5:11

76. Dreams and Dreamers

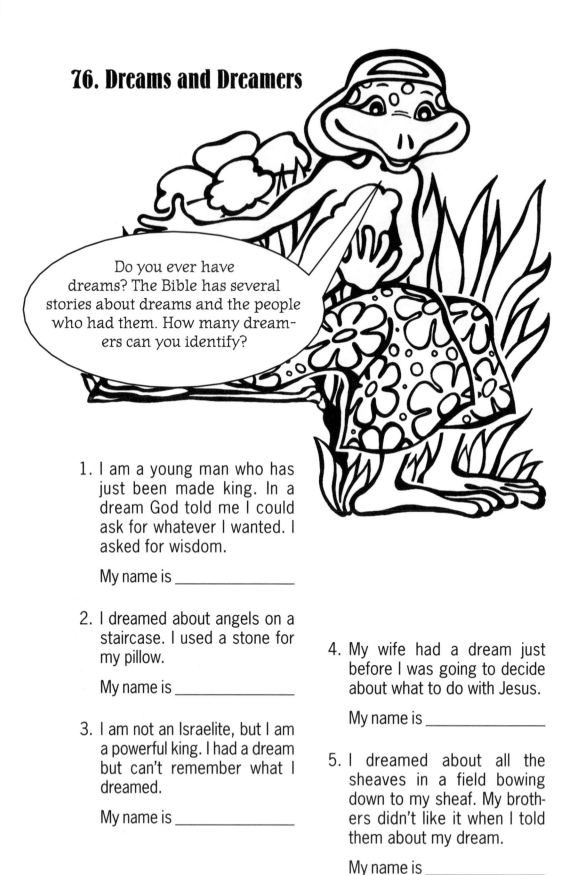

Do you ever have dreams? The Bible has several stories about dreams and the people who had them. How many dreamers can you identify?

1. I am a young man who has just been made king. In a dream God told me I could ask for whatever I wanted. I asked for wisdom.

   My name is _____

2. I dreamed about angels on a staircase. I used a stone for my pillow.

   My name is _____

3. I am not an Israelite, but I am a powerful king. I had a dream but can't remember what I dreamed.

   My name is _____

4. My wife had a dream just before I was going to decide about what to do with Jesus.

   My name is _____

5. I dreamed about all the sheaves in a field bowing down to my sheaf. My brothers didn't like it when I told them about my dream.

   My name is _____

6. I dreamed about seven fat cows and seven thin cows. I am an Egyptian ruler.

My name is _____

7. I dreamed that a big sheet came down with many animals that I didn't eat. God told me to eat them.

My name is _____

8. I was in a terrible storm at sea. God promised me in my dream that everybody on the ship would be kept safe but the ship would sink.

My name is _____

9. I saw God sitting on his throne. He asked, "Whom shall I send?" I answered, "Here am I, send me."

My name is _____

10. I saw the city of God coming down out of heaven, and I couldn't find words to describe how beautiful it is.

My name is _____

77. Who Did It?

Match the name of the person to what he or she did.

WHO

Isaac

Paul

Martha

Samuel

Dorcas

Jesus

Mary

Ruth

Jacob

Hannah

David

Sarah

Elijah

wisemen

Zacchaeus

Peter

Moses

Noah

Daniel

angels

WHAT

sewed for people

healed the sick

preached

ruled Israel

built an ark

prayed for fire to come from heaven

laughed when she was told she would have a baby

had a baby named Samuel

deceived Esau

heard God calling him

was safe in the lions' den

saw a bush burn

gathered grain

was told by an angel that she would have God's Son

sang praises to God

followed the star

climbed a tree to see Jesus

walked on water

worked hard while her sister sat with Jesus

married Rebekah

78. Birds

Several birds are mentioned in the Bible. The names of the birds are scrambled, so you may have to check the Scripture reference if you need a clue.

low	_____	Leviticus 11:16
kwha	_____	Leviticus 11:16
gopnei	_____	Leviticus 12:6
aleeg	_____	Psalm 103:5
rroomnact	_____	Leviticus 11:17
ktrso	_____	Job 39:13
troishc	_____	Job 39:13
llgu	_____	Leviticus 11:16
odve	_____	Luke 2:24
nheor	_____	Leviticus 11:19
yprsoe	_____	Leviticus 11:18
varne	_____	Proverbs 30:17
bta	_____	Leviticus 11:19
wsspraor	_____	Matthew 10:29

79. Messages from Heaven

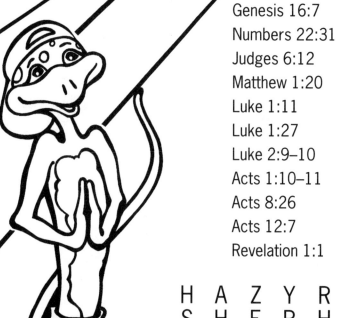

Several times in the Bible angels appeared with a message from God to special people. Use the Bible references to find the names of those people. Write their names on the lines; then find their names in the word search puzzle below.

Genesis 16:7 _____

Numbers 22:31 _____

Judges 6:12 _____

Matthew 1:20 _____

Luke 1:11 _____

Luke 1:27 _____

Luke 2:9–10 _____

Acts 1:10–11 _____

Acts 8:26 _____

Acts 12:7 _____

Revelation 1:1 _____

```
H A Z Y R A M H O
S H E P H E R D S
M A C D I S N A P
A G H A T O N J R
A A A E E O I T E
L R R D O S O L T
A E I O E L L S P
B G A P H I N I E
J O H N J A N E P
D I S C I P L E S
```

80. Reading the Hebrew Way

If you were a Hebrew boy or girl, you would learn the Hebrew alphabet and you would learn to read from the right to the left—this way:

E-S-I-A-R-P

But the Hebrew alphabet doesn't have any vowels—A, E, I, O, and U. When the letters A, E, and I are dropped from the word *praise,* and it is read from right to left, it looks like this:

S-R-P

See if you can read some familiar texts if the words have no vowels and they are read from right to left. Write the text on the lines below.

S-N-T-C S-H Y-B N-W-N-K S D-L-H-C _ N-V (Proverbs 20:11)

_____

S-N-S R R-F D-D T-S-R-H-C (1 Corinthians 15:3)

_____

S-D-N R-Y L-L T-M L-L-W D-G Y-M (Philippians 4:19)

_____

Answers

1.

3. Not Okay to Eat: weasel, gecko, chameleon, lizard, skink, rat
Okay to Eat: locust, cricket, katydid, grasshopper

4. streams, flies, frogs, grasshopper, locust, vines, cattle, hail, lightning

5. I will sing to the Lord, for he is highly exalted. The horse and its rider he has hurled into the sea. . . . The best of Pharaoh's officers are drowned in the Red Sea.

6. quail, law, wilderness, Sinai, Israel, listen, needs, sinned, desert, tiring, grumbling, God, daily, year, rain

7.

8. gold: 3,000 + 5,000 talents and 10,000 darics
   silver: 7,000 + 10,000 talents
   bronze: 18,000 talents
   iron: 100,000 talents
   total: 143,000 talents and 10,000 darics
   cedar, cedar, pine, gold, gold, cherubim, olive, gold, pine, cherubim, palm trees, flowers

9. 30 gold dishes, 1,000 silver dishes, 29 silver pans, 30 gold bowls, 410 silver bowls
   7,337 servants, 200 singers, 42,360 in whole company
   736 horses, 245 mules, 435 camels, 6,720 monkeys

10. before: 7,000 sheep + 3,000 camels + 500 yoke of oxen + 500 donkeys = 11,000 total animals
    after: 14,000 sheep + 6,000 camels + 1,000 yoke of oxen + 1,000 donkeys = 22,000 total animals

11. O LORD, our Lord, how majestic is your name in all the earth!

12.

```
D  L  T  R  A  E  H
U  O  Y  O  U  R  S
P  R  A  I  S  E  S
L  D  L  Z  I  W  O
L  O  L  O  F  O  R
I  A  E  P  R  N  U
W  I  T  H  A  D  E
P  R  Y  I  L  E  R
Y  O  U  M  L  R  S
L  L  I  W  D  S  A
```

13. The heavens declare the glory of God.

14. The Lord is the great God, the great King above all gods. In his hand are the depths of the earth, and the mountain peaks belong to him. The sea is his, for he made it, and his hands formed the dry land.

15. birds, cattle, trees, nests, stork, mountains, moon, sun, lions

16. fish, frogs, flies, lightning, grasshoppers

17. Praise the Lord.
    The Lord is my shepherd.
    In the beginning God created the heavens and the earth.

18. goes about with a corrupt mouth
    winks with his eye
    signals with his feet
    plots evil with deceit in his heart
    motions with his fingers

19. The Lord gives wisdom.
    Keep your foot from evil.
    Do not be wise in your own eyes.
    Do not set foot on the path of the wicked.
    Lazy hands make a man poor, but diligent hands bring wealth.
    Be sure of this: The wicked will not go unpunished.

20. feet that rush into evil
    haughty eyes
    a lying tongue
    hands that shed innocent blood
    a heart that devises wicked
       schemes
    a man who stirs up dissension

21. 1—f, 2—h, 3—e, 4—j, 5—d,
    6—l, 7—c, 8—m, 9—b, 10—k,
    11—a, 12—i, 13—g

22. Like a scarecrow in a melon
    patch, their idols cannot speak.

23. The Lord your God is with you,
    he is mighty to save.

24. She will give birth to a son, and
    you are to give him the name
    Jesus, because he will save his
    people from their sins.

25. baby bottle, bassinet, Christmas
    present, Christmas tree, cross
    necklace on donkey, football,
    glasses on Joseph, headphones,
    hockey stick, radio, rocking
    chair, stained glass window,
    teddy bear, tennis shoe, ter-
    adactyl, toy train set, wristwatch

26. star, savior, stable, angels, baby,
    manger, Mary

28. Glory to God in the highest, and
    on earth peace to men on whom
    his favor rests.

29.

30. Jacob, Judah, Jesse,
    Jehoshaphat, Jehoram, Jotham,
    Josiah, Jeconiah, Jacob, Joseph,
    Jesus
    Abraham, Amminadab, Abijah,
    Asa, Ahaz, Amon, Abiud, Azor,
    Akim

```
K U P Q Z C G Q U W I J Z Q Z
Z P J O T H A M F J I E I J C
C R X N W E A Y R E Y H I P T
N H A I N O C E J H I O Z I L
G L M A H A Z G T O J R Q Z M
B I C W L Q E Y A S O A X I Z
J U D A H K F N I H S M K K A
V I U B J A C O B A E A S E M
G I I B I G B Q M V P H M S M
X F B J H F O A X C H A U S I
M X A A I X W C C A N R B E N
R O U A H H U B Q J G B A J A
O H A I M A R O J J D A V F D
Z M H T H A I S O J C I Z X A
A S A O Z T S B C G I Z T Z B
```

31. age, air, anger, ant, are, ate, ear, east, Easter, eat, enter, era, erase, gain, gate, gear, gene, get, gin, goat, gone, got, grain, grate, great, greet, grin, groan, insane, irate, iron, nag, nation, near, neat, net, nine, noise, none, nose, not, note, oat, one, orange, ore, rag, rage, rain, ran, rang, range, rant, rat, rate, ration, reason, rig, ring, rot, sag, sage, sane, sang, sat, sea, seat, see, seen, set, sin, sing, sir, sit, site, snag, snore, son, song, sore, stain, stair, star, stare, stir, store, strain, strange, string, strong, tag, tan, tar, tear, tease, teen, ten, tenor, tin, ton, tone, tore, train

32. If you want to enter life, obey the commandments.

33. son, mat, people, grass, eyes, net, boat, fish, mouth, coin, jars

34. pearl, sheep, coin, garment, son, treasure, goats, lamp, bowl, net

35.

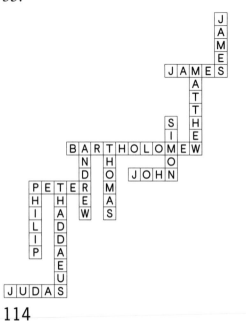

36. As I have loved you, so you must love one another.
I will come back and take you to be with me.
I and the Father are one.

37. Be clean.
Son, your sins are forgiven.
Be quiet! Come out of him!
Stretch out your hand.
Listen!

38. Zacchaeus

40. poor in spirit—kingdom of heaven
persecuted because of righteousness—kingdom of heaven
merciful—will be shown mercy
meek—will inherit the earth
pure in heart—will see God
hunger and thirst for righteousness—will be filled
mourn—will be comforted
peacemakers—will be called sons of God

41. I tell you, do not worry about your life.

43. foxes, birds, dogs, scorpion, camel, fish, rooster, sheep, wolves, snakes, doves

44. Capernaum, Nazareth, Bethany, Jericho, Emmaus, Nain, Jerusalem, Bethlehem, Sychar, Cana

45. Jesus loves me

46.

47. Let the children come to me
I will never leave you
Peace be with you
Follow me

48.

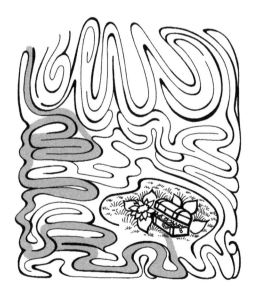

49. ale, alm, are, arm, ear, earl, ease,
easel, eel, elm, erase, jam, jar,
jeer, lame, lease, leer, lure, male,
mar, meal, mere, mule, muse,
ram, real, realm, ream, reel,

resale, rule, sale, same, sea, seal,
seam, see, slam, slum, slur,
smear, sure, use, user

50. He is risen

52. angel, stone, soldiers, Jesus,
Easter, garden, empty tomb

53. airplane, American flag, beach
umbrellas, beaver, bunny, cactus,
cattails, Easter basket, Easter
egg, fruit basket, hot air balloon,
lake, lamp post, railroad, sail-
boats, squirrel, trash can

54.

56.

115

57.

58. Believe in the Lord Jesus, and you will be saved.

59.

```
B  L  T  H  R  O  U  G  H
P  W  D  I  E  P  A  T  H
A  I  I  T  R  S  A  H  O  T
O  L  M  H  U  O  T  H  E
L  L  A  C  R  S  A  O  C
O  D  D  B  R  L  E  A  N
T  M  A  D  E  A  D  O  I
S  E  M  A  C  O  M  E  S
I  A  S  S  T  O  P  E  S
R  N  A  L  I  V  E  I  N
H  N  O  F  O  R  A  I  N
C  O  R  D  N  A  M  E  N
```

60.

```
F  R  A  N  D  O  L  D  A  Y
A  E  C  A  R  G  O  D  B  R
T  H  L  L  O  K  J  A  M  B
F  T  O  L  L  P  E  F  A  R
G  V  A  E  O  F  S  Y  O  U
E  K  H  B  O  W  U  L  A  P
P  T  I  R  I  P  S  O  C  O
A  M  O  T  S  I  R  H  C  A
O  M  A  G  L  O  H  T  I  W
P  L  A  Y  A  K  E  H  O  P
```

61. Jerusalem, Patmos, Tarsus, Perga, Smyrna, Athens, Berea, Caesarea, Antioch, Lystra, Ephesus, Troas, Corinth

62. Gideon, Rahab, Samson, Joseph, Moses, Abel, David, Sarah, Jephthah, Abraham, Noah, Enoch, Isaac, Jacob, Barak, Samuel

```
E  H  A  H  T  H  P  E  J  O
A  B  L  E  U  M  A  S  K  E
C  G  I  D  E  O  N  A  L  T
M  O  E  I  S  A  R  R  E  S
P  D  A  V  O  A  B  A  O  A
R  A  H  A  B  R  A  H  A  M
E  B  C  D  O  M  O  S  E  S
H  E  O  L  C  A  A  S  I  O
T  L  N  O  A  P  H  A  O  N
S  I  E  T  J  O  S  E  P  H
```

63. bed, been, bend, bent, bet, bid, bide, bin, bit, bite, bone, cent, cite, cob, coin, con, cone, cot, debit, debt, den, dice, din, dine, don, done, dot, dote, edict, edit, end, ice, into, need, net, nice, nine, nob, nod, none, not, note, notice, tee, teen, ten, tend, tie, tied, tin, ton, tone

64. The Lord is my helper; I will not be afraid.
Never will I leave you; never will I forsake you.

65. ache, age, air, ape, arch, are, cage, can, cane, cap, cape, car, care, carp, chair, chain, change, chap, char, cheap, chin, chip, chirp, crap, each, ear, earn, era, gain, gap, gear, gin, grape, grin, grip, gripe, hair, hang, hare, harp, hear, hen, her, hinge, hip, ice, inch, nag, nap, nape, near, nip, pace, page, pain, pan, pane, pang, par, peach, pear, peg, pen, per, pier, pig, pin, pine, preach, prince, race, rag, rage, rain, ran, rang, range, rap, rape, reach, reap, rich, rig, ring, rip, ripe, ripen

66.

67. If God is for us, who can be against us?
God is love.
This is love for God: to obey his commands.

68.

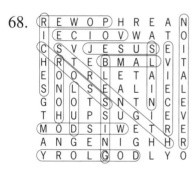

69. air, ale, alive, alone, ant, are, art, ate, ear, earn, eat, eel, elevation, elevator, era, eve, even, ever, into, iron, lane, late, leer, let, lever, line, live, liver, lone, lot, love, native, near, neat, net, never, not, note, oar, oat, oil, olive, one, ore, oval, rail, rain, ran, rant, rat, rate, rate, ration, rave, real, reel, relate, relation, relative, rent, reveal, rivet, role, rove, tan, tea, teal, tear, tee, teen, ten, tie, tin, toe, ton, tone, tore, train, travel, tree, vain, vane, veer, veil, vine, vote

71. 1—66; 2—39, 27; 3—31,102; 4—Esther 8:9; 5—John 11:35;

6—Psalm 119; 7—Psalm 117; 8—Pentateuch; 9—Proverbs; 10—Jeremiah; 11—Obadiah; 12—Gospels; 13—2 Thessalonians; 14—Luke; 15—2 John

72. 1—Gideon, 2—moon, 3—praise, 4—voice, 5—alarm, 6—Lord, 7—dead, 8—heard, 9—angel, 10—blast

73. 1—12, 2—5, 3—2, 4—3, 5—2, 6—3, 7—5, 8—7

74. coconut palm tree, covered wagon, dolphin, fish, lake, monkey, mushroom, parrot, pine trees, seaweed, snowman, starfish, stream, walrus

75. apes, rabbit, dog, foxes, camel, jackal, horse, ox, lamb, pigs

76. 1—Solomon, 2—Jacob, 3—Nebuchadnezzar, 4—Pilate, 5—Joseph, 6—Pharaoh, 7—Peter, 8—Paul, 9—Isaiah, 10—John

77. Isaac—married Rebekah
Paul—preached
Martha—worked hard while her sister sat with Jesus
Samuel—heard God calling him
Dorcas—sewed for people
Jesus—healed the sick
Mary—was told be an angel that she would have God's Son

Ruth—gathered grain

Jacob—deceieved Esau

Hannah—had a baby named Samuel

David—ruled Israel

Sarah—laughed when she was told she would have a baby

Elijah—prayed for fire to come from heaven

wisemen—followed the star

Zacchaeus—climbed a tree to see Jesus

Peter—walked on water

Moses—saw a bush burn

Noah—built an ark

Daniel—was safe in the lions' den

angels—sang praises to God

78. owl, hawk, pigeon, eagle, cormorant, stork, ostrich, gull, dove, heron, osprey, raven, bat, sparrows

79. Hagar, Balaam, Gideon, Joseph, Zechariah, Mary, shepherds, disciples, Philip, Peter, John

80. Even a child is known by his actions.

Christ died for our sins.

My God will meet all your needs.

Betty De Vries served as senior editor of trade and children's books at Baker Book House for more than twenty-five years.

Donna Greenlee is the founder of Greenlee Designers, a commercial design studio in Grand Rapids, Michigan. Her work includes book covers, illustrations, and packaging for publishing houses and other commercial clients.